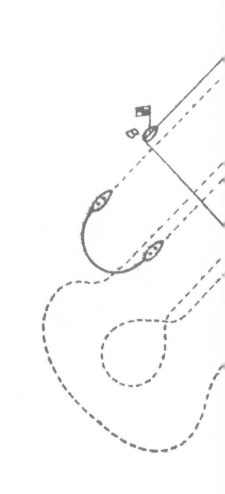

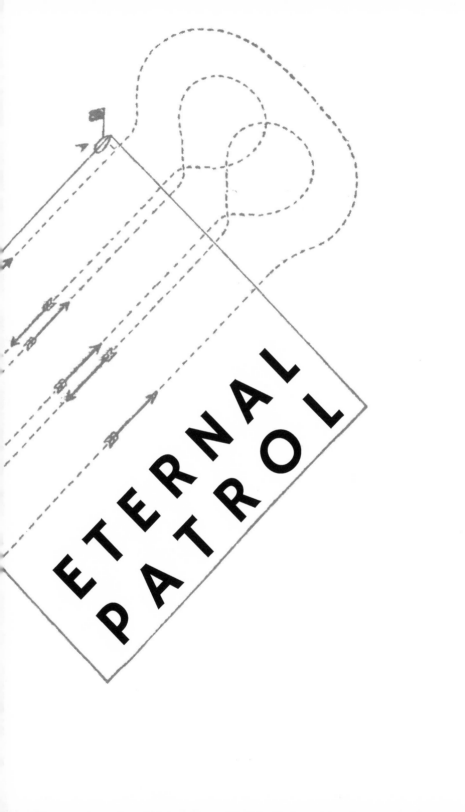

ETERNAL
PATROL

ETERNAL PATROL

RUSSELL DILLON

FORKLIFT_BOOKS

FORKLIFT BOOKS EDITION, August 2013

Copyright © 2013 by Russell Dillon
ISBN 978-0-9995931-1-0

Edited by Matt Hart
Book and cover design by Eric Appleby

Cincinnati, Ohio
www.forkliftbooks.com

MY ABILITY TO BE FAR AWAY IS NOW ONE OF MY GREAT SUPER POWERS, AS IS BEING COMPLETELY HEARTBROKEN AND IRRATIONAL WHILE CRAVING MANY OYSTERS, SEE ALSO: INVISIBILITY

We are desperate for more mercy, please. The waves, pulling themselves further apart like the molecules of kerosene upon my skin. You can try this at home at your leisure, but the itch stays. Somehow, we remain related to water, and there is that feeling that stays with us, very similar to the way we felt, when, walking out of the Newest of New Museums, it was as though our hearts had been bleached. Similar to the way the number 5 is forever changed since Jasper Johns, just like the way I learned to use a word wrong so long ago, and now cannot reach to it. It is forever changed and beautiful, and so resembles plungers and dead butterflies. You'll have to forgive me, similar to eating a meal you don't enjoy, but has been served by someone loving. Or you don't. Or aren't, but you may just be nice. Sometimes, I forget that you don't see everything I see. I imagine we're the same, and that you might not understand yourself, or me, or the drawing of an atom; it all seems to stick and stray and resemble a topographical map of the imploding whimper we surround. We want what we want at dire ages, and often die still wanting that. So I am not mistaken, please remit my personal units of measure so that they may remain true before the Empire. A gas station in New Jersey was accidentally delivered jet fuel after the hurricane, which you'd think would be more exciting, but in the end it just made cars break down. Often, everything will surprise us, like the way all things on this planet need sun—even, and especially, those things that never see it and are furious.

CONTENTS

for James and Grace Dillon

&

for Stella, Lucy, Lorca, Agnes
and the next ones

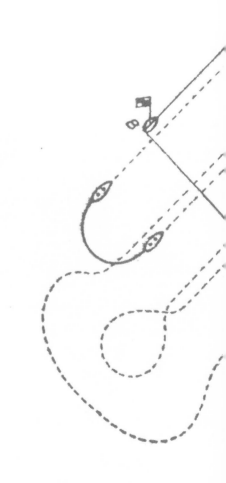

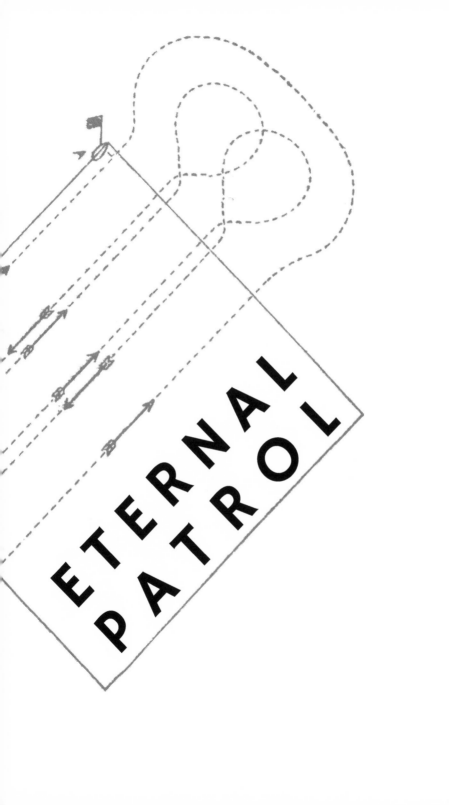

THE CYCLIC NATURE OF THE MIND

In September, the trees pass
death notes to each other.
They read like any amorous
letter, "I love you, I'm sorry,
we're all dying, come back."

These sentiments are precious
because they are perishable.

The snow shrinks into itself
until it's forgotten
what it came for, the ground
forever writing the story
of who's been here
and who's coming.

Reasonable, yes, but less than
we've learned to want, really.

Spring's conclusion,
"Fuck, fuck, fuck,"
which can be a good idea
but that's Spring's answer
for everything, so it's hard
to know when to listen.

"Take off your clothes. I would
like another drink, please."

"Would you like another drink?"

"Please. Yes."

EIGHT DIFFERENT TYPES OF PLAID & MY
BLACKOUT THEORIES

Enter us, lovely, you true machine, and trace
shadows with your scalpel into one more moment
we're stealing. Forever and unmercied, these lives
elsewhere, with the hope to fold some paper seven,
then more times, while in our veins, this new viscosity.
One more thorn for the beloved, and a balance upon
new mist. Being a person is quite difficult, especially
in the face of a tape recorder. All night I could hear you
speaking about these recipes for breathing, yet all morning,
there has been nothing but the dark air of this song.

LATE DAYS OF INVENTION

Un-can some matter, and immediately, *Woo-hoo*,
but still, we beg the question, "What do I do?"
I may never know, and that too is a begging
in its own way. You can no more stay awake
forever than you can be scared of the thought that
turning-in can reset everything you've just learned
to love. I have little concept of this, the easiest
of machines. All of my lies about repair will be
found in my prolific ruin, and also in these designs
for a spray can to administer dust to the immediate.
If I could just lay here long enough, both you
and the sun would come back—just you and
the Ice Age. Just me lying here, and even that
is improbable. The vehicular agent in my canned-
dust is a fear, propulsive and nearly detectable.
The dust: imported and current. Moments stain
ink upon some winds we may never feel, but can
purchase remotely. I can't believe in anything
at all, which is why confessional poetry is never
too far from the surreal, how it's all just object
eventually. This tiny damage, and how we can't trust it.
This everything, this dust, its stillness, and its fixity.
This day after days, and the ones that follow, patently.

TINCTURE AT FULL BLEED

Someone must be here, because I am talking.
Because I hold congress with the wind, and there is no sound
that enters the dark. I'm breaking down before your bottle structure,
witness to the ways we've worshipped glass just to give up
its secrets. Sunset again, we say at dawn. Looking back
we see what little distance we've gone, indentured to ballast
and folly, to you in my paws, clawed-animate. Now alone-er, turned
fierce, and I am disappearing into the mild drown, as from all sides
I is overcome. Bright hatchet falling. Only now to ponder,
full of blood, dumb poses. Thoughts about hunger. Theories
unsurpassed by reason, abandoned, and sometimes we swim.
Sometimes we thrust ourselves into other worlds just to feel
slightly more alien. Draped sails and a light rain. No way for
all that moon to dress, entirely, this patch of water. Blowing
back from, then in, and into. Against these ways we were never
        warned.
One man writes the same novel about redemption one hundred times,
yet his wife remains dead, their fight unresolved. Tomorrow, I will be
bent on some reclamation without an excuse for the present. Our lives
which were their ideas, our stories which were their stories, told
        drastically
of love and of searching, told from comfortable homes, and told
        to no one.

DEXATRIM SONNET ON A EUROPEAN VACATION

What a beautiful life. My room
so full of gorgeous-yet-filthy
clothing while I exclaim everything.
What I wear is plaintive,
and no less ragged than me. I'm not
very tough, but I am unafraid
of the physical manner of barely
existing. You alarm me, but so
too make me entirely alive,
small lightning. I walked gigantic
distances this evening, yet barely
to you was I closer. I touched my hand
to my face, and nearly felt tired.
I looked to you in a stranger.
From there I felt tiny, then relevant.

SCRAP/METAL

There never was a picture. I was
painting solo in the robot lounge.

There was not one dance, and many
shoes went unused. Hot months

of no restaurants or public steps.
The strings of the instrument

continue to get broken, but song
does not stop for any machine.

The assembly line revolted, stirring
backward through their coffees,

finds the one thing we're actually
breaking. In the sequence of the pick,

the limb-free, claw unsure. Crashed
autos now unpaint themselves in flame.

Boats strip back to music, sink into
names of new enemies. The value of a fossil

in our ash one day quits—stays perfect just for
nothing. Now we rally back to liquid, lecture sand.

UNDAMNING DAMAGE

In the lost-shore droning of my mother's house, I pack
shotgun shells with my baby teeth and go hunting in old corners.
Dancing in a long-dead light without rhythm, where all of our
fire has been friendly. Let the trumpets now address us:

between two bridges to one island among rivers, I wake,
and nothing has changed. What has become is hidden,
and some hours are shorter than you think while you wait them out.
Also, life is shrinking, which is as evident as dawn's infringing
　　　　trademarks.

I look up at the sky, and we are everywhere. Lonesome, possible
with everything—though reluctant—we allowed the boy to die
in your arms. Natural, he and all the struggle, lugging
the air of us to forage within his flame-flimsy body residue.

Into you, I tunnel from the past and now we bore into these stains,
dress nervously in the pigments of his burial suit—its straw, water,
and smoke all dissipating. As ice crystals swathed in dust undo clouds,
we must also unzip from these shapes and into our final slivers.

Beneath the surfaces, we urge not to bend within this thinness;
our creeks, taps, and whispers placed beyond the inner ear, beneath
the sea, like a hand asleep in our centers now waking and hungry
to feel everything as a fist. Once buried, now I do not know

what I see, what is out there, though I am frightened. Ringing
     fearful
of the next sound, with my hand in the soil that's becoming of my
     family.
We dig and we plant and in the next season find half stones, an
     old, broken
arrowhead, the smallest fray of rope tinged with blood and
     unnamable knots.

EACH COMBUSTIBLE FLUID OUNCE IN ITS DIVORCING

There was something nearly traceable
within us, horse-like and holy.
Without this field, there would be
an unnamed vacancy between trees.

That last time I saw you I nearly
drowned, dancing at the fountain's edge,
a tent pitched upon rock beside
my piano and a lazy beggar's cup.

Here: A photograph where your face
is obscured by blurring snowflakes.
Gloam-lensed, a moment before
inviting me into your papier-mâché home.

I'd forgotten to say *never drive through Texas
alone* and *touch no drought with your
runaway hands.* I too was consumed
with unfortunate left turns, roads abutting

former lives, their phone lines, their calls
without warning. Small houses evaporating
in your gas tank, whole instances becoming
merely vapor, exploding listless denizens.

Maddening how, in this home, in this storm,
I fear most the lightning and not the rain,
the improbable over the certain. A sound
from the map room: mellifluous, stupid river.

WOULD-BE DAFFODILS

When I arrived here, I was given
the box of everything I had previously
loved, and was reduced to ash in the process.
Drowning in this, the concept of
a dark so foreign it's as though light
could never be familiar again, and here, there,
in the rainstorm all around us, some gutters
runneth ran over while the earth curves onward.
I refuse now to be fooled by the magic of spring,
the false and the lovely, its betwixity of blossom.
You, once, a candescence of vacuum in the glass
stroking midnight, the sand ringing morning.
The flower that would be, were it not merely
the crocus, the instigant, the warning. A world
which is beautiful, but as charts read, failing.
All of our best dawns can be rewound
into a blinding inertia, an early bedtime.
A rock formation weathering now resembles
some celebrity long forgotten. Once I saw
a clergyman in a photo-booth. Once
I saw this cement-mixed hallelujah.
Eventually, we're inoculated for the apocalypse.
These aren't flowers, these are flowers responding.

SELF-PORTRAIT IN STYPTIC PENCIL

Landscape, apothecary.
Ungather us now, come loosed

and chanting something orphic.
Unlikely, and then hermitted

in weather's full broadcast.
Each ghost preserved

in a specific mouth, stretched
further to fiber, missing muscle

unto bone. Small mercy of dirt,
scarred strange, as now, and

of maps, the mountain stars, the one
hundred ways that they're saying,

"goodmorning" in the palace,
making mirrors out of everything

and its prisoners. Such victory,
historic, sweeping diamonds

from all this and its crematorium.

REDRESSING THE MANNEQUIN AT DAWN

It was here, waking in this body grown
wild around the idea of myself, where,
despite what the commercials have promised,
my body smells only of skin and what leaks
through it, the ghosts of every tiny animal inside me
nibbling at the controls. I recall the grand ballroom,
your daughter's voice on the phone like a gavel,
how she said hello as if she believed we weren't
on some kind of rocket ship, inexplicably.

It was only then that I wanted to apologize,
with a regret rarely directed outward
as an oar is pulled toward *we*, the rowing.
As algebra has evaded me since the bricks
have left the building site, how I imagine
a way the dust will settle in a structure,
a fawn catching its hoof-print upon the thesis
of some clover, and a honey bee abiding.

Admittedly, on my best days, I am a specter
trespassing through the dusk of a borrowed landscape;
a dog ripped from its post, dodging traffic.
This is how I re-imagine the lexicon of gone wrong:
the night fogs on with its horn sounding,
my grandfather's toolbench, the outline of a

hammer traced beneath its hook, both gone for years
and the jam-jar of tenpenny nails, relieved greatly.

Show me again your face, and the trick where
our bodies cast shadows not their own,
and how in the process a light escapes.
I've spent the long day watching a short life's dream.
A baby deer crawls into the expensive sausage,
though I can sense a world where its horns grow on.
This is how I've twisted in the vestments, complacent

in the aftermath, Saturn ringing in its orbit.
And me, a warble in the nectar;
one finger in the dark, manufacturing passion.

THE EARLY THEATRICS

There were few ways to fail then,
but they were radiant, unique ways.
A cathedral, not an hourglass.
Everything, when viewed
from the proper distance,
exposed its seams, but those tickets
didn't come cheap. Sometimes
it's the assurance of light that develops
sadness; others, a dim uncertainty.
Erstwhile, the full house.
Erstwhile, the head and the body.
Erstwhile, cha-cha-cha.
Candles in the orchestra's pit.
You never wanted to sing
before they wired the mouth shut,
but after that, the desire was terrible.
The term "opera libretto" must be
changed to "dramatic and tragic
poem set to music," though no one
will really notice. With regard
to flight, the two greatest challenges:
creating the device and concealing
the device. Occasionally in the music,
it's great silence that's most appropriate,
though more often the exaggerated crash

of metal and feather dusters. If anything
is forgotten, it's bad form attempting
to regain it. Always smile. Pretend
you know what you are meant to be doing.
When the curtain rises, you must
dance the fever of your legs disjointed.

VOYEUR'S THEORY OF THEORIES

The truth about a boy alone is anyone's
passing wonder, but most theories agree:
you are all I need, spoken to everything in a whisper.
He spends a lifetime trying to stop
sending letters, then slows like the cinema.
Once science succeeds at fractioning our liturgies
we'll be outsourced to strangers. Our ancestors,
with their own version of wood betraying nails,
move their story from high sea to swollen depth
in an abruptness of woe. No governess, yet we feel
the emotional pang of some theories, and these are
true like everything. Sometimes, dervishes in
the evergreen, then nine eels tied together as a team-
building exercise dreamt up for god. No test run.
No Rorschach. No coffee stain. No equilibrium
anticipated in the de-oxygenation of a turtle
in the centrifuge, or in the quiet moment when
a bored world's population honors their potatoes.
You know you should, but you don't, with nerve.
Even when a friend chooses death, we can't be sure
it was a fair fight, so now must avenge his life.
From here, deconstruct this warm problem of the human
condition of soul derision. How long that first map
took to construct with drops of blood, still centuries before
we came up with *You are here*. Next: the New York

School, meeting all over the place, then passing on
the key to survival, which is: fuck a kaleidoscope
in Paris, followed by moderation. And now, my friend
is too scared of the windmill to ever fully dump truck.
No one cares about the batteries in the flashlight
until the power goes out, which is a metaphor for *May I
have the number of your therapist?* I felt so entitled to
love that song before it was popular, and now only
within elevators. One joy of the dead is anticipating
no horizon, then there's the surface grief of never finding
a significant replacement for the coffee table. Badger
teeth in my dream again, yet I'll sleep through one more
blizzard. Seaside, and all the ships built out of electric fencing
like they own it. Now look, you can't even see your hands.

REVOLVING WINDOW

All you need is a good set of horns, then this
banging becomes the right kind of tragedy.

I can't believe it's us, either. I'd argue, but
there's too much evidence with its retorts.

I'd have missed everything, had I not once seen your
eyes unfold from their ornate shapes and remain paper.

I'd do anything. Make my lists slightly shorter,
and upon checking, "everything" just below

"construct shorter lists," I'd abandon them, too.
There're so many varieties of rescue. Its mesh

so loose. So many gloves neglected and for each
an other that is loved, an other often longed for.

It's a matter of time, mostly—one clock slows,
while another remains, ticks completely atomic.

DON'T BE SHY

Be anything this evening. Be here, but don't
        be a voice knowing anything
        other than the impossible
language of "yes."

Be rain, and be on the window, or the window
        in rain, but please, be no
        further than breath in this storm,
or the storm of breath spit dumbly

on your neck, and please, break entirely
        upon the shore of me,
        little rancher. It must be
raining in so many places, but why

and who cares about that? Attendees
        of many tasks would happily
        trade with their colleagues,
but never would they wish

to eclipse any less of this star
        I am shot into, the shadows
        of that last Sunday morning
not loving you. Don't be anywhere,

please, and never again shall you be sent
        waiting in any tongue.
        Be not shy, or timid,
in the air
all around me, and also be no further.

MORE MID- THAN -WESTERN

Let's get something straight: the quivering bolts
of your empire portray a certain innocence
but are not nearly a match for the fits of your sky.
Yes, the four doors of the heart fly open, slam shut,
though the motion's symbiosis is never quite explained.
My hands had forever wished to steady themselves
beneath the moon-ladled gravity of your breasts,
still I could not utter one sentence of that prayer.
The eyes hold the hopes of a parent's squandered
pension fund, only lack their faith in weather.
In the revival tent, the potential for salvation
was husking itself into shout and semblance, yet
the town dried flat-cloudless a month later.
Still, there's my pallored envy of the tumbleweed,
its misfitted agreements to orbit in obscurity, then:
Somebody get this tongue some teeth! Oddly enough,
not even the all-night gallop of rain can express
the sky's dumb desires to tap upon just one umbrella.

AGGREGATE LESSON IN SWIMMING

I could all night wonder at the two stars
we are, and the funny way we attempt
to rearrange ourselves into a new kind
of constellation, though there is just one

straight line being drawn between us,
in every direction, no matter how
indeterminately we walk together. We shake
bones to the wind and continue, curious as soil.

All of my faith is the laughter in a root still
thirsting for the drench of a thing I could not
yet provide for us. Faith as a wing in the drench
when work is what happens arid and crisping.

I once watched almost everything burn, and still
I could not conjure one kindled strand of water.
Living terrified of the sea, I had no way to keep
myself from drowning inland, truncated.

IMPERIAL TREMENS

No surprise that we're here, but surprise
in arriving. Being dumb with love and studying
its pastures, we linger and imagine the clouds
without trousers. In rain, we all break. A bit.
As everything in nature breaks from its purpose,
succumbing to agencies of splinter just to spite us.

In sleep, we live and strive to remedy
much older mischiefs. Though I rise and braid
trees, turn lovers into strangers, I still cannot
wake up in this life. Let's get awed in a world
where there's everything and always we feel missing.

We're all hopeless, and that's the single way
we don't resemble our shadows. Even
when memories kaleidoscope beyond these
worn lemons in shrinking light. Each day
you are a leopard, but worse than that,
you are entirely a giant mouse. Go figure.

In the highway of our Mason jars, we break
down and beg for assistance. Drunk, our friends,
and stupid, playing happy. Brilliant, sick,
too strange at how they're stuck and sad, yet lively.
Gasoline in their veins, and we all feel electric.

So much blood in us now, we're a terrible fortress.
When we're wrecking our landscape, it's our
radiant fence. I'm masochized to throttle begging, *join me.*

In the one dream I don't admit, a girl walks
out of the forest, and she is dancing. There
is no music, and we are not there, but the trees,
the trees are ridiculous. And in my real life,
after the woodgrain of the ballroom has forgotten
our swayings, our mistakes, our drunken ricochets, and all

of our crowning movements—the tree still remembers
its felling. Your spills, your admissions, your missteps—
without the right music, everything is personal.

COLLECT CALL FROM THE HAGUE

I called you so I wouldn't call her,
late in the night and conscious
of what was not there, though outside
the loosely knit world spun asunder.
Even then, my broken glass was imagining
new ways to be hammered back into the mosaic,
your tempera dry in the bottles, cracked.
After the art museums, we obsessed
in the world of scrimshaw and fraktur,
only later to discover we did not have
the occasion, nor the whalebone for either.
And then there was our great envy of the painters,
how it all became an agreement with our sisters,
that light alone would reveal their breasts
to be our mothers' breasts, like a map into
the backstreets of a small town burning.
There are terrible places in this world, but
people know our names there, so we return.

SECRET DAMAGE

Welcome to the re-instatement of corporal beauty.
Welcome to the well-arranged room, the shallow gorge,
a moon in its wispy vespers, rampant, and the dream
I have had about your body for each night of the recent age.

Here, a tin bird, rusted by specific rainfalls, exacted through
the bronze cage bars. Do you still anticipate, at least,
a tiny earthquake? Us, adrift in the orchard, shaken in
the middle ground: fruit to the earth, that bird to the sky.

I apologize. I was darting. I was shifty. I was shaking
in my feather-suit, preening by the water's edge. The myth
had been the human being, the being becoming the mythical
and look, I am invisible; unwatch this bad dream waking.

The man, born fortunate in his shipwrecks, rows solely
toward a deserted island to atone for the luck in his life.
He carried the last of the love notes, not in a bottle,
but tacked sturdily to the naked mast, his useless wooden leg.

This, the story from when I held the king's favor,
this, the narration from such fickle gallows—I will miss
that horse most of all, how he believed, again, in a humdrum
ecstasy. It was my belief in the otherworldly astronomers,

my love, and it sealed my fate. The way our world blinks on,
blinks off in their eyes. I am sorry for the metaphors I've tried
to live and make a life in, and how I've tried to take you with me.
I'm sorry for the way I become a boy in each stranger's hand.

Welcome, again, to the cloistral nature of mishappenings,
to the maelstrom of the equine, to the big empty world of oceans.
My light, this morning, appears broken, and yes, this is the
small sound I make in the world and how I timidly step away from it.

Once was, when she whispered a simple thing toward the sails
it set forth the boats, and I remained, the navigator on these endless
lesser journeys. I am sorry, as the ship's log reads; as it punctuates
the orchard, so punctuates the ocean, the horse, the plainest of
        English.

THRILLED, NOW

and if there were a siren that sounded
at the hint of our underground desires.

and if there were a way we could wander
crooked as the unfletched arrow flew.

and if there was a moment when the wind
blew back all we blew into it, if that inertia

existed, if that night were more night-like,
if that girl was more me-like, if the prose

was more lifelike, then yes, these glasses
could be more like my own prescription,

would I need a prescription, but were fashion
more than fascination with some other self

I would sound, somewhat, different, from
the highschool girl I hear in my head swearing

the next one will be the best prom ever, for certain.
but what I'm saying is a life grows tired in the station.

a train waits as long as its passengers, then no longer.
a difficult concept for one whom the doors close upon.

if we all have a mother, than why do we not
all have gloves pinned to our sleeves, maternally.

if I storm through the desert, is there not one blossom
wondering why it's diffusing the frequent atom of our absence?

the tension of the bow depends on arm's length,
though the center of the target ponders none of this.

I enjoy couplets, only because I
witness a third line evading reach: heroically.

I'm uncertain of waking, though the day is there.
I'm unclear of meaning, though I quote freely.

if Kenneth Koch could see my house, he would
be ecstatic, though (most likely) not about my house.

I love him, not like a father, but like I saw my father
love him, and then was helpless in every situation after.

I love him like I love Marina, as though I were
Marina and, as if again, it is 1957. as if I played

the piano, just once, perfectly. and with that chance,
that a thing could, just once, be perfect, I'd ask

where have my mittens gone? my mother?
my hemoglobin intake capacity? the ice cream?

could one man share the bus with one man,
where then, the need for a bus? a rickshaw so inhumane

not one of us arrives in any true place. a wheelhouse,
a photo of steeple-chase reminiscent of grandparent stories.

if I could love one thing as much as your absence,
it would be the wake of you, the morning leaving.

if there were a time, the time would be hellspent,
mercurial, wasted on a couch whilst I wallowed.

I don't mean to hyper-extend my vernacular,
but I've always thought you were hella cool.

through my thin, wispy curtains, I hope
I can see more than can be seen in return.

if you could say one thing in two lines it
would be much more than one thing for two lines.

this is my problem with form, the problems
it forms, and now I am exercising.

I dislike few things more than poems about poems,
or about writing poems, or about silence in want

of poems, because to a degree, every poem is about that,
even the ones that are screaming otherwise,

the way that I scream otherwise about most everything.
I love you, I hate you, I wish you would have collected

the dry-cleaning, whereabouts I mean, I wish the dry-cleaning
could have been me, that I hate the telephone, that each sound

outside of my window is a reminder of the saturation point,
the moment where each person breathing forgets about science

and lets what science screams become our mutual inadequacy.
if there were one thing in this night, I'd hope it to be you.

that and a humming-bird's skull dipped in bronze.

REAL ESTATE

If not for the comedy, I would be lost
in the trace-wells within the bird
of prey's eyes. Done in by the combine,
but who hasn't been sought with their attention
diverted, so often, by a beautiful machine.

I'm not going to lie, I want, please, very much
to see your breasts, to cry while you don't touch me
at all, which will be argued through therapy
as issues with my mother, but I also want you
to bury me in her garden, never telling where I've gone.

Untelling her was the only thing I ever wanted.
She, who gave me this mouth I have since lost
the instructions for and so have been using
improperly for endless days. I was embarrassed
when she found me in the process of disemboweling

our family's one good seahorse, wailing
in my life vest. I would be lost, to this day,
were it not for the butterfly's yolk, my shiny metals
skirting beside her rose bushes in August again.
Out there, I am middled, growing downward

'til I hit the ground. Somewhere, I promise you,
there is an entire empty house, its dry breath
filling each secret. Within this place, her
tepid respiration consuming every corner,
accountable to no one, inhabiting each tiny room.

READING OF THE MINUTES: POSTCARD CONVENTION

I once decided not to be a cowboy—
decided tap-shoes over spurs,
grew trees deciduous, inverted.

Forfeited. The inability to hold my breath
forever, proving me a poor candidate
as the next submersible deity.

With small respiration and large intent,
you parade through the costume box,
extract the plastic crown, begin weeping.

From our heathenous origins
we congregated thus:
The Laying On of the Handcuffs Ceremony.

Having sewn myself into a suit
of flame, I emerged from the water
bleached, rotund, belching chlorine.

Can you recall that day, its dream of time
and how we strove to restore the statuary
ruined in these spaces set between us?

Please refer to the matter of deoxy-
ribonucleic acid separation, slighting
the chromosomes. Misunderstanding you.

P. S. Here's a small amount of everything.

ORDINARY GREEK

Oh rainy day Olympus,
your sight is marred
and so deeply betrothed
to the ornamented spectacular.

We have the holiday;
we place animal in animal
and then become more
animal ourselves, consumptively.

All that age has given me
is a perspective roughly
three feet above my former
youth, with less will to wonder.

Men wake, and are woken
to an ocelot, an uncooked breakfast.
We would like to go home now.
We would prefer a slice of lightning.

APRIL 1ST, HUES

Outside my window, it is eighty degrees and the no more
rain of a tactile eternity is enacted by a crow diving
repeatedly for a hawk in the lower levels of all-sky.

There is no more rescue, no more milk in the refrigerator,
and no way to reach beyond my full-length blindfold
into the world of the eaters and the hungry, indiscriminate.

I am so close to the lonesome, and the sun pushes this
further into question. All of our reviews palmed
slick between passing, untracked but to keenest eyes.

I am just inside the window, next to a world, and you
have to believe me, the edges stack and stray apart
in just this way: all appealing as a passage for everything—

startling itself in our many versions and definitions
of attack, of defense, of the sky required to break you.

WHILE PACKING FOR THE TRIP WE WOULD NOT TAKE

After the Rapture does not happen for the fourth time
we recalculate the glisten of our expectations,
we unregister our former beliefs, reconsider the big
dance routine. We elaborate reconnaissance, tear
the wires from the plaster, the fat-fuck faces glower
"Oh!" in the bonfire. We try to buy our children back,
try to un-combust and remap the course toward end-days.
It is possible a thing can just go on, though it won't.
Long after we do not ascend, but have ended ourselves
amicably, the tires of our cars live on within air pockets
of their own making, forcing themselves to the surface
of the garbaging fields, to the surface of the topsoil, the bluegrass,
the groves of eucalyptus gone to fire. I've heard each car
tire is one long molecule, but like us, it will still burst
in the UV of a world perfect without us, though always mourning
our expectations. Geology concedes to vacuum, concedes
to star power, careens long, deep into the double helix
of our mutual unfolding. If origami is one art, so too must
be our undoing, as here, in our paper-cuts so much citrus
will not consider the other fields and groves. Beset to hives,
burned down to a liquid, we are nearly half tarmac sped into
apocalypse. God. Now. Remember: the poison and its antidote
are both synthesized from one mother venom. We can't deny
that. Its logic, its simplicity, and the grace with which both
slip soundlessly into our blood and continue to end everything.

PRELIMINARY HEARINGS

The one contract I would like to negotiate
regards not being forgotten in both worlds.

Begged between kisses, sounds like a great deal, but the
time that exists between those kisses is never divulged.

While I consider the stars, a city unbuttons
its blouse, revealing two bridges seduced to glow.

Dear you belonging to an empire I am without: I
now understand the need for such strength and wall.

The water at my feet, so necessary for my arguments
with the strongest of flowers, betrayed by errant weed.

Drawn from the smoke, one interviewer submits
their interrogation of form, sketched in carbon.

All this ice cream melting, another party ruined by progress.
Now a whole crew of shadows hammering back at the light.

THINGS THAT SURVIVED MY FIREWORKS STAGE

I may never love anything as much as the flame
        that denies me, or the action figure so real,
        I dream to sleep in the manner of the plastic.
That, and I, too, burn

this and your four other selves, despised for
        their hidden and strict membership policies.
        A satellite drowned in tidal pools, unwound
around a clock divorcing its hands. Estranged

is a word I have given too much away, having
        found more, then less, of my parents' future,
        its brush strokes, idyllic numerologies and
a fundamental need for subtraction.

The litany of cats, blinded and faithful
        to the rough tongue we saved for swearing,
        and for the ways we've found to burn
in these placid, empty spaces.

LESSER KEY TO CELLAR DOORS UNHINGING

I'd never wanted to feel this, your noticing. Please
disregard my uniform and return to the unnatural
motion your body took to when crying. Days when
the pipes shook their rust in dull, reticent sympathy.
Days gone empty, wandered. So many days, and still
only this house, creaking, absently the family long dead.

Even when the family is dead, and you are
sitting in the basement, possessed, here, in
the darkness of *nothing* and its affiliates swarmed
and surrounding you. Rotting brick, and everything
you eat here tastes only of that, so what's the point?
Beneath the ground, even the spirits of the lawn

on this long, gray morning are shocked down by rain.
It slows, stops, and continues to draw upon a space
unoccupied. Don't waste your time with surprise.
There are angels still falling everywhere, and they see
your breathing as a recognizable mischief. All day
you hold silver through wind and its attachment to sky.

Strong effort it took to cop one pill to get holy,
yet still I'm surrounded by demons, their latch-keys
insatiable. I must not lose the desire to make love
to dirt. Risking earthlessness, prime event and tragedy

bound, grown prison-ed with the song and hex-tongue
vowing never to surrender light in the little I repent for.

The little I still repent for in my resurrections, reborn
again to live as Cat. Reborn once more, to lumber as Toad.
I disharmonize my sixty-six voices, and still I am not
counted among men, fingering through a pocket full
of ash. I know I will burn everything down, as before.
In the spaces empty, left behind, I am only to split smoke

swimming through darkness. This basement, small hammer
in hand, chipping everything to its porcelain vestige. We are
coated in the dust of it—filthy, naked, begging for a new
flood, never wondering, "Whose hammer had this been?"
before exhausting into sleep, still gripping it, cowered. You
notice, as the flames begin, you may have nothing more than endings.

Remember that thing that guy said in that movie one time?
Yeah, me, too. Remember that cup game with the string
where you rope-burned your cheek? I remember the chase.
I remember the way I laid my bicycle down less and less
carefully each time, and I remember how I've done that
with everything ever since. Once something is marred,
it is unresurrectable. After the first scratch, nothing
is new. I remember trying to seem smart on a phone with Heather
Koch, knowing things about her name because of a mayor
and this was New York. I also remember faking the knowledge
of Nelson Mandela's release, and how I learned to make myself
more wounded because it felt good. That was 1990, which
doesn't sound so far away, because I've tried to learn and instead,
have forgotten most of what I'd intended to love. I've met people
I'd meant to carry, but I am tired—already forgetting to miss
even this.

INSTRUCTION FROM THE WEATHER MANUALS

Begin again, as is whispered through the rubble,
and soon you, too, must take notice how
we have come to be the spark of shaved ice
upon god's dulled skate blade, though depending
on your text the deduction may be more
to the effect that our existence is
merely a glimmering, frozen seduction
within this storm and all its merciless dreaming.

In other climates, a ladder slips from the roof,
revealing nothing more than extinction and
an ability to translate its form into theory again.
Not much snow hides the so much everything,
later, revealing it as even we begin forgetting.
We, these dim martyrs, pray vested in the shadows,
and that ain't good scar-lighting. Hence, the narrative
about how everyone we love is dying; inscrutable.

One more tale of the man on fire, one more tale
of a journey, no heroes, and me like a stranger
quarrelling with stars, coming to recognize
neither the sky, nor my hand upon it.
Undeniable, we are all so precious, and now
we pause to give back your name—old lover,
old namesake, old cloud still greeting me in this mask
constructed from this witchcraft, that heat, these meltings.

EVERY FERRY LEADS HERE

We forgot the hostage
on the auto-deck.
The horses were falling apart.
One more nautical mile, then
pacing the land in three directions.

Normal vehicle movement
is entirely far from normal,
and the sailboat receding
into the distance
  could have been anything. Access
to the auto-deck and other levels
of heaven at times will be denied,
and for this: no cure.

And here is where the bartender
tends to show up, her arms
two loaves of bread, her arms
full of olives and flowering dill.
So as not to bruise the mint, parading
in the wake, we switch to licorice,
stencil flowers in the salt. Apply
  now for surrender.

The crustacean that is this
version of union extends
its knobby claws to you
and sings its song, a lullaby
in the shape of a wave. So sway
with tendrils and barnacles.
Here we are, between two shores
and also, we are oceans.

And also, we are this house
that lets ships remain unsunk.
And also, the hostage has fallen
away, arms pinwheeling a bloom
of joy. This shore. This is where
rest meets the long, soft work
of the sea. Now and then found near
the beaches, pebbled and lapping our one
true fire, alive right here, upon the docks.

RESIDUAL DAMAGE

Before you are tested for what's wrong with you
you will be tested for the thing that is fighting
what's wrong with you. This comes to pass
and so I am intubated with geraniums, set
to dig a hole beneath some poorly measured
gallows. All of the bayonets have been stripped of their leaves.
Bleak, these days, the ghosts within ghosts and one more
shade set to dimming as it outlines its everything. The water-
hung air, the single missing note of each song.
There's a static in the waves and how it crests at our
desire for the classic sound—building thirty new
technologies to achieve it, then laying down to cradle
the days. Come astonished to the window, once more
in the gleam. Gather shadows, swirled in pools to wash
our other shadows, trace each motion in the dark
with tools made of coal. That day at the boardwalk,
in the booth taking our photo accidentally, blasting
a stranger's fingerprints into the cartoon of your bones,
and before that day, when the repairmen apologized for free.

DUMB-KAFKAN

Mid-day, and I wake writhing in this body of an insect.
I mean idiot. Intangible dreams and the coffee all wrong,
one useless foreman handing out the rocks we must carry,
and my brain cartooning everything next to new beauty.

Heirloom tobacco and a compass in the sky. The islands
that are not too far, yet we know not how to get there.
Probably by boat, but we and all we know are constructs
of stone. We and all we know are jealous and harboring.

Midday and a continuous waking. My lion is just watching
me. My lion means these eyes behind hair, still sleeping.
My lion means to growl, means to mean it. Hot water and
a fog barely lifting. I don't think you can see the bridge out

there. I don't think this means we're not connected by a
tether of string to every tiny insect buzzing. I mean bumbling.

PAST-PERFECT-IMPERSONAL

Dear you in all poems, who is forever unnamed: hello again.
I believe in you and you have defined in me this age of witness.
I too was born into a wicker chair surrounded by laser beams,
praying for the least strict of virgins. Strange, both of us now
so afflicted by an illness's fluorescence, and how, from its post-
    morning
confetti, we stagger like shadows longing for their authors. Would
if I could, other, but I am approaching you like static, masturbating
my heart in this strophe of light. There are many versions of how
I fell asleep vandalizing your gardens, but I beg you: Could it be, that
all of them are true? *What is it you're unable to surrender, and please,
may I have that,* is how every love letter can be summarized. Another
is *I am sorry we both fell for the idea of our grief,* but even that fails
to explicate how you hold me by the edges as we dip past
    everything.
There will be no way to undrench the oceans, but is it possible we
    might
become those clothes we can't recall falling from that one time
    we never
truly met? How lovely to imagine all of the bones in my ear existing
only for the possibility of you saying *hello* in forty different tongues,
rather than fearing some dumb bear's invitation to dance emerging
from the darkness, and both of us so delicious. In my simpler speech,
I am sparrowing for you, though in fairness, I should warn you now:
sometimes I sleep face down in the world, others face down in
    the ether.

UTTERLY CIRCUS

The sun is rising in Cincinnati, and this is of note.
Different times, always, we inhabit, and I fear this
is the wrong direction in our collective biographies.
Categorizing the missed chances, the people we are
that don't resemble one another. I am in a borrowed
room surrounded by a child's toys. In my blood, enough
antibiotics to start something fresh, kill something wrong
I've been chasing. These hands, arthritic and broken
into the tiny lines of the dumb pugilists. Late night
corners and their boxing fractures, dancing words back
to me. It is completely back to sanctum, and the drugs,
they tear my guts apart. Incidentally, I move to become
better at happening. Sometimes attempting only to get
more dead. I say, "utterly circus," meaning nothing.
My friends, they've been so kind, and I live in a meadow.
Love in the gasping. Lash in the wind, and lower
the sails. I look for you now, in the bouldering sun,
so much sawdust and residue. Enumerate shadows
of the demands we've put on light. Why did we ever stop
mopping? Mixing the chemicals that become deadly,
though we're never sure which ones, so we become adept
at holding our breath, and we hold it indefinitely, which is how
we learn what is clean enough. Gleaming like a postscript
to the zombie apocalypse, and everyone walking around
like a broken heart still means something. If we've got fears,
what are they? I've got a guy, a guy in one circle of nothing.

I IMAGINE THAT VOICE IN THE FARMHOUSE IS YOURS

There are a lot of voices in the night
when you don't live far off and alone,
and this may make you feel more alone.

Often, I think they are saying great numbers
of dumb things, and sometimes, radiant degrees
of brilliance that I cannot comprehend. Rarely,

to me, can I imagine these voices aimed. It is quiet
and I am desperate for some information I am
without and crave deeply. Someone is yelling

to their dog, at their lover, and I am neither.
I am not inclined to answer, but I wait. I don't
listen, but I anticipate, maybe, a beautiful voice

one day calling, not to me, but to *Come here.*
I won't know how, or to whom they're speaking,
but I do believe in that echo. I will feel ready.

INVARIABLE MASS AND REACTION

Even now, looking back on those
days: atomic, heat-swept trace
elements in the silence of men.

The mostly broken cars
pounding deaf our
wind-rung ears, a new liquor
caramelizing the dry bone
of tooth. It seems hard
to remember

anything but the stars,
their brilliant spin-art, and
yet some echo washes
audibly in the annals
of a pop-top memory.

Coasting over the bridge,
a car full of boys
breaking each other's
hearts beneath a lucid moon.

Pushing back in those seats
of errant need, I'm sure now,
that we said nothing.

Not the names of our fathers,
no audible insult or sexual falsity.
Not one turbulent syllable.

BOY WITH THE RADIO-PHONIC HEART

Of course there is a better music.
Think *march*, whisper *sonata*
and you will know immediately.

But who was I to choose
this clamoring transistor?
Who asked me if I wanted
the din of a hollow chest
in continual broadcast?

Walking the roadsides
at late night, too dark
to tell the difference
between heartrending
and heart-rendering.

Do you honestly think
I would choose to know
that six-measure rest
prefacing each love song?
That moment in the stalled

engine of cricketry, on the
porches of Milwaukee's
indigenous male populace,

counting out the quiet
by thumbing a dent
into twelve hollow ounces?

Sure, it made me popular
at parties, I'll admit,
but where do you begin?
How can you ask her
to dance when each time

you are hushed? We all
love this song, but come
closer. Move too much
and it's a different tune
altogether.

On the news it's always
the most spectacular meteor
shower of our lifetimes,
and each morning,
we're obliged to agree.

CASTING LIGHTNING

Don't be overzealous.
The gods are half the myth,
the other half is the believing.
Better to start small.
Though you can focus on streetlights
for an entire evening with
little effect, so too you may
glimpse the sky for a moment
and the whole pin-cushion falls.
Eat your vegetables.
Before you write a word
you must demystify all
you've read. It is advisable
to start with a garden, annuals
first, perennials as needed
to fill the earth's vacancies.
Mind yourself, son.
All the world, a variation
of rain, even the desert,
which is most rain-like
when the winds have stilled.
Each moment, the residue
of our greater moments. Each
moment, the dream-life
of our lesser moments.

When building temples
you start from the ground,
you end with the temple.

PHANTOM STATION

Come one, come gathered, and come hither with the remnants
of an alternating current and the residue of ancient pill bottles
powdering our veins. Come again, resurrecting from one
line to the next, photon to photon and waves of sound,
strings still tattering our fingers like a clothing worn within us.
Unraveled like water into gravity, and back then, to water
tending gravity, away from, then back. Back toward the rooms
and the de-stricted floorplans previously intended for dancing.
Come back again, and let's all lay down, just forever now.
In surrender, we may be stained, inglorious before breaking
to the patterns we inherit. Come, clouded and irreverent, come
once more, the broad leaves and their ridiculous thirsts, washing smog
from its hands and a whiteness that we beg for, then beg to ruin.
If you will, we can return to a little girl shouting, "hello, bird,"
and meaning it, the little bird birding back, nothing. Follow me,
and we will return to the red triangle with all of our misinformation,
and no one will be able to stop freezing in that surf. None
of us will be able to collapse any further, the molecules origamied
all the way back to sacred paper. I will wait here in the phantom
station, and exhibit how we all have called for an absent transport.

ETERNAL PATROL

There will be no return, and you've not said goodbye.

We dive, and break surface, just as juniper
breaks into gin, just as wine haunts on as its former
grape. Often, everything, on one unending course.

But I know that's untrue. And you know our maps
extend to the edges of unthorough imagination.
It is romantic to be beneath the sea in a time of war,

yet these hopes are overdue, presumed lost.
Stern-rigid difficulties and an imagined apology
for things we've submerged beyond seeing.

The air, and its oceans, they want to break into you.
I'm bringing this, and my ignorant translation of light.
It is Christmas morning. Your mother is crying,

and so are you, both trapped or dead beneath this ice,
within these pressures, these peekings, these tiny bits of glass.

DAMAGE DAMAGE

A horse throws its shoe, and all over is the sky.
I have been given a lot of drugs lately, but have taken very few.
I never feel the weight that I am when reading it from a scale,
but oftentimes the weight that I feel goes unmeasured.
There is more and more in my past, contending and conscious.
I can still hear your voice, and describe it as "normal wear and tear."
Percussion, combustion, and how we decimate one thing
in order to produce another. I have been produced this way
and only I am able to witness these traces. Every fifth round
in my combat situation is illuminated, and, though it reveals
my position, it also informs my aim. Loss and harm, a depletion
in value, an occasional hindrance to navigational properties.
Seeds, water, and good soil, yet still the earth does not roar
when we slam into it with our shovels. Rather, it resists us by
not turning. On one side of the bridge there is a suicide view,
on the other an out-to-sea-ness that is attacked by larger boats.
These tasks, and everything about finance, are quite foreign to me,
but when the fires start, I understand completely. Some people
can accept no less than burning; some grains, no less than distilling
in their hands. Born into blossom, then spreading out and falling
from our half-lives, our thrusters, our re-entry negotiators
and the communication devices we construct for their irregularities.
I've raised all of mine to the air, and I can't stop talking about help.

TRAVEL LOG

Believe me, please, I too have been on roads
imagining the assorted ways no one like me
had ever stepped upon that pavement
only to be passed by someone so like myself
I become ashamed for them. It was excusable.
It was the age when raindrops weighed a ton
and we could not stop ourselves from weeping
when the wasps wore out their motors, and then
more sadness when they could not begin again.
You led me into the empty house where
they collected their wounds, cataloging
the false starts and the poorly-salted meals.
It was the time of night when everything is heard
as a gunshot, even your leaving, my imperfect
marksman. Your charters: revoked. Here,
in my reduction, I have cut my teeth and venture
forth unnatural. I'm a man and the flowers are
in bloom, shunningly. I must confess, darling, this
whole time I've been sitting on my stairs spitting
paper into puddles, and nothing is reflected; come over.

(DEAR PAUL)   VERMONT STARS

Not one thing in this night will lie to you.
The clouds, hiding their purpose beneath
the stars, then the stars, hiding their light
beneath their unshamed reflection of lightning

bugs. They dance like the recombinant DNA
of some lost god, searching for his name at sea
again. Here upon this bench, we have no reason
to be so alone, though I've needed you quite desperately

to be a silence. Now, loud, and how the rains begin.
This, too, may be seasonal. Extravagant. Misting
beyond the dreams we discussed; drunken, then
triumphant, as at dawn we trek large, separate ways.

How we part so haphazardly, as though some risks
could have been less tragic, then tap-dance this slight
divulgence of safety and its snipers across our one, true light.

FALLING TO RISE

Wake up in the garden alone again and wonder
about the long life of seeds released to wisdom.

There's not an aephid [sic] alive considered worthy
trade for the speculative tone of water-boarding.

The subtle gouache of your aesthetic is a new motion,
and the committee has decided to call it *guantanamoism, etc.*

We're leaving nothing out, because that's important.
All we've included is a scaffold to be removed, like darkness

when the light is all we have. To offer anything less is what
can't be spared, is a measure nevertheless, and soon we're all

dirt again. What we'll never see is the future, as our heroes
have all mortgaged the past and its homes. With these capes

the wind seems more than brutal. Brutality is what we say
when we say everything else like it's a sweetness.

LAST ARTICLES

Please let this not be the same prayer failing us.
Let us not remain hopeful, kneeling before whiskey
and the ghost that grows within our mother's
hands. Kneeling beside the crucible of our beloved,
tempering our failure as a new way to pay attention.

Sometimes I dress only in oils, imagining the breath
we've given each other blowing back, as if the world's
balloons have been awaiting their secret plan to deflate,
our history of concealments now demanding explanation.
Hold not accountable the rising in us that will not settle.

Come back and be dust among us once more. You, too,
will be asked to defend this song someday, so please
hear the appeal and grant us a vernacular to define
this barrowed longing. Do not construct, nor catalog,
that other empire's pillars in so many more wrong cities.

Try. Howl as you may or may not like. We cannot, as we were
promised, be begged back from ash, but desirous of this process
we dreamt awake and were anointed terribly. Plied thus, we lie
like deconsecrated jungle gyms, like a daylight astrology unhinged,
like a canopy of not much foliage obscuring us from so much moon.

POSTCARD AT THE DAWN OF ICE WINE SEASON FROM A LOVE-STRICKEN VINEDRESSER IN GERMANY WHO ACCEPTED THE COLLECTED POEMS OF FRANK O'HARA AND JOHN BERRYMAN'S DREAM SONGS AS PAYMENT FOR LODGING

Dear not be sad Henry back homing,
Hello from Mr. Bone! You all night
drunk couch not filling,
yet. Come lost again
more book! Feet hardest
to ground all year, all leaf
Lana Turner for good. Sky making
faster burned cork of night,
no talk in a truth of sun, so much.
New sleep make not nightmare
of girlwant! She make all
Coke having call "poem" for
no name word live stronger.
Now air break puddle, me to hill
in lantern hand for icegrape.
No more lean to you door, (what
john 5 spot?). When not looked
will dark fruit press tongue
to teeth to squish like
say of her name. What
eager door to tell for note!

SHOULDERED

We were set upon, we were hoped for by strangers.
Sleepless on the roadside, where the god-ship would
not save us, where the bus-lines did not stop, and friend,
your shelter was aflame again. In accordance, we turned
our attention to the sea, which relentlessly attempted to
give back, resulting only in a deeper interest, much like
the delicate hands of a woman refusing to welcome us
and becoming more impossibly beautiful in doing so. You,
my friend, who became so adept at the sadness such events
would seek, and therein continually illustrate your capacities.
Ghost-pitching your fists through the nightmaring glass,
your father reflected behind you re-inhabiting the vacancy
of a torn mare's eye—watered, trembling, yet stilly fixed
upon the meadow's gypsying heart. As we must, we send
word with the carrier pigeon in our usual midnight syntax.
As they must, those uncertain birds head south, unsorry.

POEM FOR ST. AGNES THE TINY, AS SHEEP

Unwieldy we are, in these suits, in a chill and patient.
Patient, in your tongue untamed, and me in my meager,
manger ready, sculptured and reticent toward the oratories.
Soon among rough ashes, and you in your tiny and your roar
chanced through a California, a garden with its wet-resting guests,
and the idea that a thing will not just go on. This lullaby
of surf, half-babies, and the *argent revelry* being dreamed
in unspun wool, one person's disbelief convexed in fog,
brooded and wronged in it's honeyed declaration of being here.

Though we are supperless, though the *heart was otherware*
and you are infinite, dragging delicate, an infant in your claws,
your tiny, a frock among the timbrels, and we with your *lambs
unshorn*. Spill of ocean spinning, so frothed and thoughtless
as this tedious fountain, citadel of our dear forest lineage
collapsing all around your tame, your latticed and loomed,
your one burning school house, the tiny, initial venture.

Girl-saint, sweet conjuror, languid as the silkworm drunk
upon spindling mulberry, wonderous with love in the nest
of unharmed eggs, fanged discovery of the feeble, and we are
wearing the mask of the gentle. *Never on such a night*, wind
unfolding, and your tiny, your station, praying *never leave
my grace*, growing dusky in the tall grain we've raised for these
days of fire. Legitimized, our adornments, the *ring-dove frayed*
and how we're weaponizing our hearts like a *tongueless nightingale*.

Let us, please, remain in your tiny, your reserves, our memories of the knot-grass and where we keep the secrets of monsters, their tales told, their twilight and the dwindling grace of old bed clothes. As a dim martyr, I have knelt in the garden with its legion of shadows, amazed by your hair, how it lays half-hidden in the school house each child intends to have fled. Share with us, the constellation of tiny bones trembling at so many distances, fatigued in the listen to your soil, *though a rose should shout* and gather new stations of dust.

Approach once more, and as if for the first time, entranced in your tiny, the wind in our shearing and your *empty dress* stirring noiseless through the paradigms of the *half anguished*. Gather this, the new sleep of breath in a world so lavendered, a speech loomed, your claws and your lucent, a colony of stone and the shadows unyielding within your *glowing hand*. Redeem the fabric, the seam-work grown agitated into garment where the thimble, dreamingly in your tiny, has changed and *I know not where to go*. Again, I feel the frost wind blow and I fear for your garden, the sharp sleet and the night-song finding me worse than one *rude infidel* on his first morning, finding no school house.

Prepare me, woolen, for these lessons, though *there are no ears to hear, or eyes to see* the shearing of the hungry in this village, glaring. Fathering the wet, now frosted and chosen from its flock, not the dyed, but the darkling found untamed in its suit, like us, so urged to make a *human sound*, though our mouths remain unflattered. Your tiny, your roar, and only from me will

you inherit this *huge empty*, its bolts and hinges, its rogue steam
and the ages of storm where I dare consider paradise, its simple
tasks of *shade and form*, how in these suits, unwieldy, and here,
we will gather ourselves together amid the thousand unsought ashes.

NEXT TIME, WHEN THEY CALL YOUR NUMBER, WHAT NUMBER WILL IT BE?

It's a work in progress, like undressing
an angel. Sometimes you focus so much
on the wings that you completely forget the party hat.
Also, it is difficult to stay warm in some instances.
More difficult, still, is to walk through them.
Stepping down from your crucifixion is never
easy, but just think about the next guy in line,
then think about stepping into that next line
and having no idea what it's for. Not one of us
will survive untouched, and more to the point,
none of us will survive at all. Sometimes you get
re-geared in the watchmaker's repair salon for dolls,
and others, restrung in the National Sewer Union's
Annex of Non-Musical Instruments. Sometimes
you have no idea what you will miss, and then
you see that next person in line behind you,
and you are struck entirely by their wonder,
struck just enough to fake a little of your own.

EXIT INTERVIEW

Please be so kind as to break your needles
as you exit the sanitarium. Just one more
version of a life ecstatic—that, and *you
can't take it with you.* Even the lake's
letting loose its bodies, dreams non-recounted.
Pooled ink and magnet particles. Our ever-changing
script undressing from its quieted warnings.

Hey, Tiny Minute: how rapacious your
discarded manuals. Neither you, nor
the lamb will do too well with this one—
sun pitching its fists upon one last gasp
of snow, the undone world fractioning attempts
to fold itself over, and your body in its sands,
pressed cold against the windowed heat.

You, too, will not escape unravaged, cupping harm
all around you, the light fraying on in an old-fashioned
way. Genome-d and disseminated as the stars, how
they've wandered, dressed in your metals now
staunch and rusting. It's happened hundreds of times—
halcyonic in the giftshop, weeping upon snowglobes
that slight pause of warning and what it's not yet told you.

COLLATERAL DAMAGE

Goodbye, silhouette of my hand to the sun. Goodbye,
monster image cast back upon my face, and
good luck to the barge exiting port in its ore of light;
its crew, its cargo, and propellers so large, yet
completely obscured for the journey. So long
to the brick factories and mortar farms of
our elders, to their robot spirits and some particles
being accelerated to a celebratory discrepancy.
I will miss you morbid tractate, your skepticism
and your septic rose collection, the Museo de
Basura and the gleam upon its half-finished promenade.
My apologies to the undone planning committee:
please forgive me for the shadow upon the ocean
cast by almost everything, and moved toward darkness.

"There is a silence when the radar turns
its circles upon circles in despair."

—Tomas Tranströmer

BLED INTO SEPIA AND THE JESUS YEAR

Blessed are we in the stamped tin
and our homemade particle accelerators.
We, on this one small shelf for years
and holding onto it, exhibiting fear
unabashed as a lion toward its Christians.
With only hunger, I am saving the fire from
old photographs, to burn those saints with other things.
A bug's tiny atmosphere of windshield, the thresher
tearing one more late season's harvest, then stopping
to enter its new life as tetanus-inducing plaything.
From these morning doorsteps we raise the sun,
the deep plastic of autumn which makes even
being here a crime, never certain we will actually live
much among the willows and the unmoored boats,
the broken chains and the tyranny of the aquatic.
You may follow these rules or shatter,
fall like the sky for rain or like blood for
every cloud of wolves undressing by the tide.
Whole moments possessed by an uneven temperament,
the throne of my tiny king and his matchbook kingdom,
where one can remember when we both made mistakes
with those lifetimes, where now there are monsters
retiring beside our dead parents, magnifying
their hurt with our own, their ledgers of Braille
and the early accounts of spills before spills

were so importantly hushed in the senate
of antique dreams. Now, the one tiny rocking chair
at the forest's edge. One branch between a bird,
the frequency of matter, and an embarrassed boy
with the need to obscure. We are running
toward a transitive closure, then expansion and what
we touch we are becoming—the ambition
of string and the perils of salvation, how
it leaves our loved ones in smokey hope when
we should have just run from the flames. I surrender
now to the age and its theories, acknowledging how
one day we will look back, and seeing how lost
we are, and once were, forgive nothing for its pain.

ACKNOWLEDGMENTS, THANKS, ETC.

Thank you to the editors of *Alligator Juniper, Big Bell, BPM, Forklift, Ohio; H_NG_M_N, Incliner, Interrupture, Lumberyard, MiPOesia, Parthenon West, Tight, Redivider, The Saw Mill,* and *5A.M.* where versions of these poems previously appeared.

"The Early Theatrics" is for my sister, Amy Jane Finnerty.

"Poem for St. Agnes the Tiny, As Sheep" is for Agnes Hart. The italicized text is taken from John Keats' poem, "The Eve of St. Agnes."

"Every Ferry Leads Here" was written on a series of ferries with Chris Martin and Mary Austin Speaker. It is an epithalamion for Andrew and Nora Hughes.

"While Packing for the Trip We Would Not Take" was written in collaboration with Adam Fell in San Francisco. Its counterpart/ counter-poem can be found in his collection Dear Corporation,

"Lesser Key to Cellar Doors Unhinging" was written for the CS13 Gallery show, Hail Satan, and corresponds to the assigned demon/deity, Baal.

"Things That Survived My Fireworks Stage" was written for Justin May.

"(Dear Paul) Vermont Stars" is for Paul Mazza.

Very special thanks to my mother, Linda Finnerty.

With love, and in memory—Alice Hunt Rosanes.

My teachers, my vortex, my edge-walkers.

Thanks to Matt Hart, Eric Appleby, Amanda Smeltz, Tricia Suit, Ed Ochester, Dobby Gibson, Dean Young, Bob Hicock, Tony Hoagland, Rachel Simon, David Daniel, Peter Jay Shippy, Mary Ruefle, Glenn Patterson, Kenny Graham, Kevin Hamilton, Joey Hafner, Henry Lewis, Brandon Josie, Mike McIntosh, Matty Conway, Tim Scarpa, Mary Austin Speaker, Alexis Orgera, Adam Fell, Evan Commander, Andrew Hughes, Nate Pritts, Curtis Perdue, Javier Zamora, Jen Woods, Chris Mattingly, Ben Kopel, Mike Krouse/Madrone, Lacy Simons, Chris Salerno, Eliot Treichel, Paul Mazza, Jason Morris, Micah Ballard, Patrick Dunagan, Sunnylyn Thibodeaux, Eric Raymond, Laurie Saurborn Young, Joseph Gilmartin, Jason Grabowski, Mike & Mary Anne Cowgill. Also, everyone from The Bennington Writing Seminars, Squaw Valley Community of Writers, FTC, ba'sik, and Everlasting Tattoo.

Thank you to San Francisco, for everything, and to New York, for everything else.

Thank you _____.

Lifetime, Kid Dynamite, Fugazi, Sam Beam, Will Oldham, Glen Hansard, Big L, Gang Starr, Wu-Tang.

Thank you, Grace & James Dillon.

Jason Shinder.

ABOUT THE AUTHOR

Russell Dillon is co-editor of *Big Bell* and author of the chapbook, *Secret Damage*. He began life in New York, continued it in San Francisco, and now continues it further in New York.

Made in the USA
Monee, IL
29 January 2020